THE SOLDIER'S FRIEND

WALT WHITMAN'S EXTRAORDINARY
SERVICE IN THE AMERICAN CIVIL WAR

Gary Golio
Illustrated by **E. B. Lewis**

CALKINS CREEK
AN IMPRINT OF ASTRA BOOKS FOR YOUNG READERS
New York

December 1862

War was raging.
Brother fighting brother. North fighting South.
The country—the *Union*—was breaking apart, and
Walt felt like he was, too.

In all people I see myself.
—Walt Whitman, *Leaves of Grass*

America—it was everything he believed in.
Friendship, equality, and freedom.

His poems were love songs to the land and its people.

For Walt, America was more than a country.

It was a star, shining bright in the world.

Only now it seemed to be burning itself up.

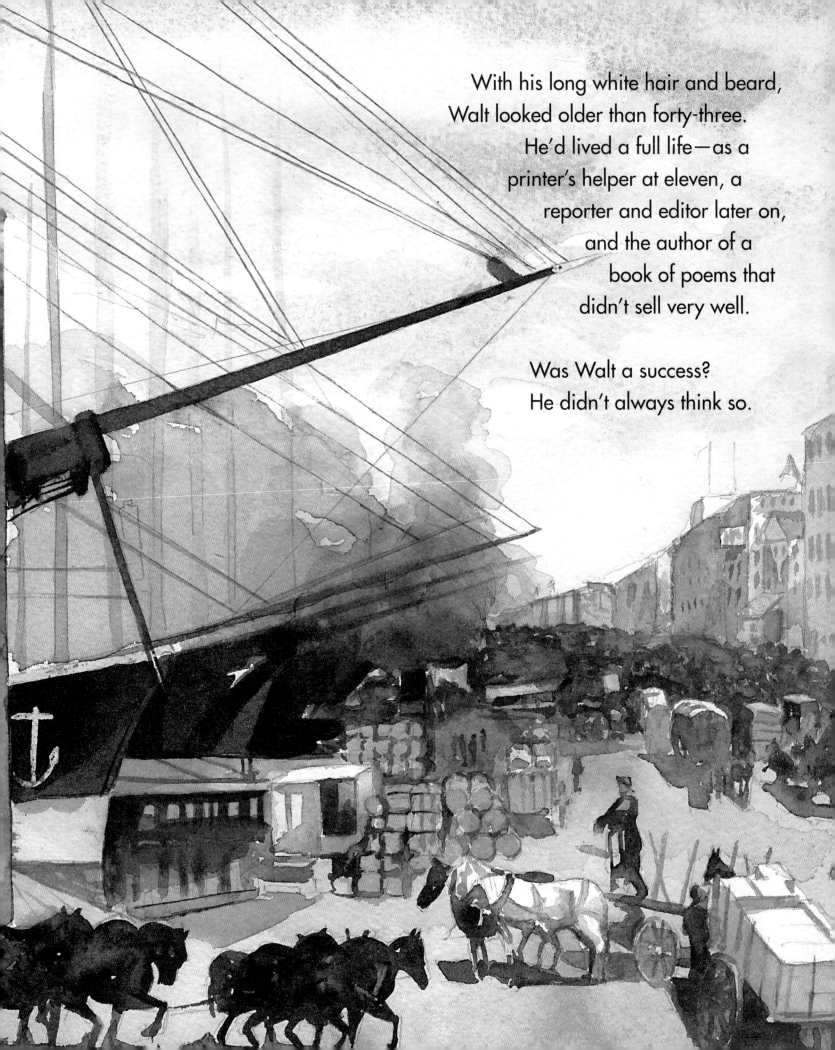

With his long white hair and beard,
Walt looked older than forty-three.
He'd lived a full life—as a
printer's helper at eleven, a
reporter and editor later on,
and the author of a
book of poems that
didn't sell very well.

Was Walt a success?
He didn't always think so.

Walt loved taking the ferry back and forth from his home in Brooklyn to New York City, talking to anyone and everyone.

He was friends with the boat pilots, and visited them in the hospital when they were sick or injured.

Those same city hospitals were now filled with
Union soldiers, and Walt visited them, too.
He brought sweets, newspapers, a kind word,
and helped the men write letters.
Small things, that meant a lot.

A lifelong New Yorker, Walt believed the North's cause was just—to end slavery and keep the nation united.

He imagined Union soldiers coming home as heroes,
arm in arm, flags waving, heads held high to the cheers
of roaring crowds.
Songs would be sung! Poems would be written!
It was a beautiful dream.

But each day, Walt read how thousands of men—some just boys of fifteen—were dying on the battlefield.

The war hadn't ended in a few months like some people said it would.

*I could never think of myself as firing
a gun or drawing a sword on another man.*

—Walt Whitman

And then, in a newspaper list of wounded soldiers was a name—*G. W. Whitmore.*

Walt froze. This had to be his younger brother's name—George Washington Whitman—misspelled!

He quickly said goodbye to his mother, and left Brooklyn for a train headed south.

Walt spent long days looking through dozens of hospitals, and finally found his brother in Virginia.

George was fine, in good spirits, with just a slight wound to his face.

Only he was one of the lucky ones.
Thousands of others had died in the fighting, their bodies
still lying on the open ground.

It was hard for Walt to put words to all
he saw.

For days he walked the camp, talking with
wounded and weary soldiers, and writing
letters for those who couldn't.

He even helped bury the dead, men and
boys he'd never know.

After dark, Walt drank in the stars and
breathed the cool night air.
He stood under the moon, its light falling
softly on the battlefield.
And he set down his thoughts, on little pieces
of paper tucked safely into his pocket.

There was so much he didn't want to forget.

January 1863

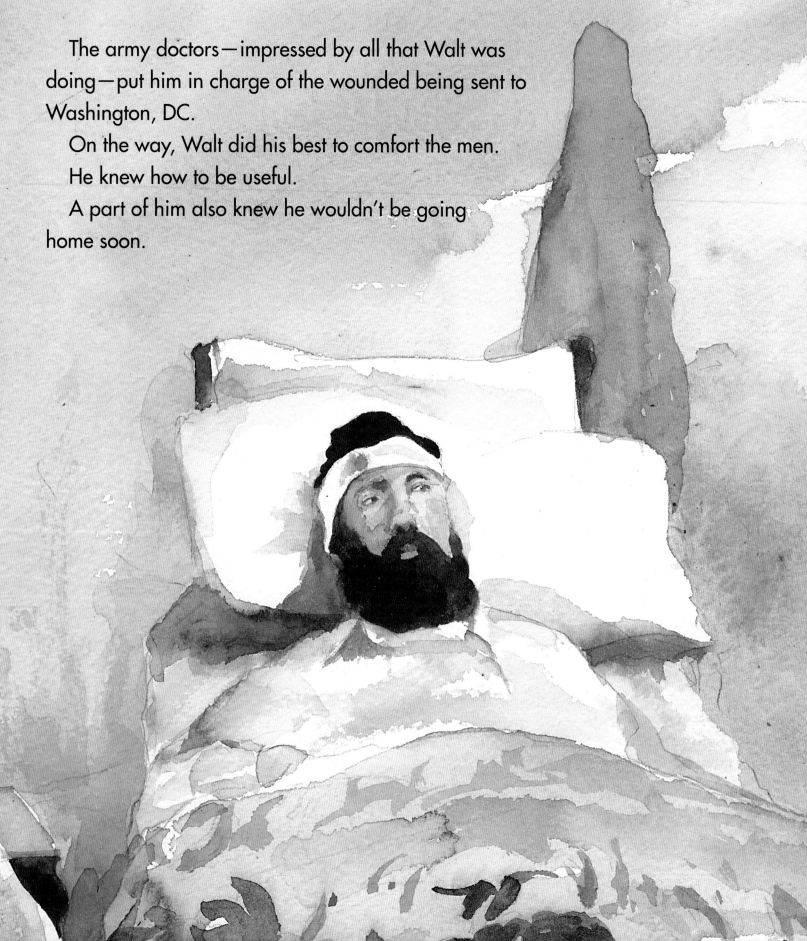

The army doctors—impressed by all that Walt was doing—put him in charge of the wounded being sent to Washington, DC.

On the way, Walt did his best to comfort the men. He knew how to be useful.

A part of him also knew he wouldn't be going home soon.

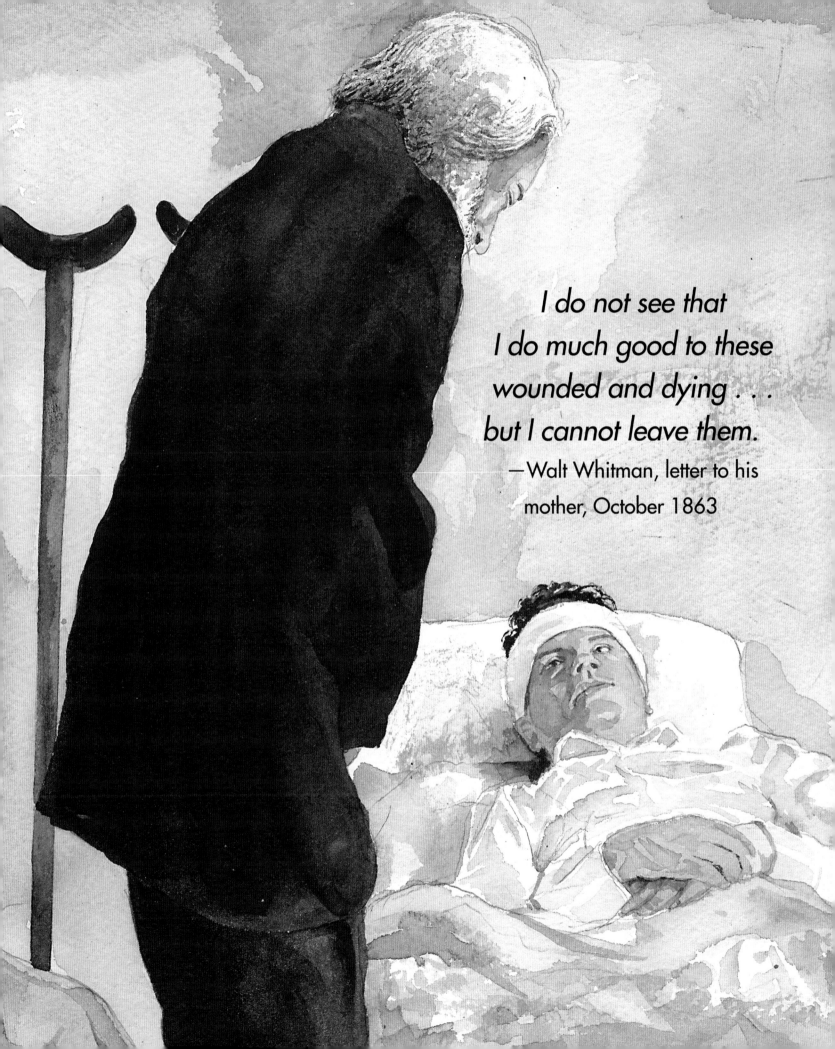

I do not see that
I do much good to these
wounded and dying . . .
but I cannot leave them.
—Walt Whitman, letter to his
mother, October 1863

With help from friends, Walt got a part-time job in Washington and took a room there.

The city was full of muddy streets and the endless banging of workmen's hammers.

Hospitals were being set up everywhere, and it was hard to tell if the half-built Capitol dome was going up or coming down.

Every day, after a morning's work, Walt made his way to the hospitals.

He tried to be strong, to be cheerful, to dress nicely. He wanted friendliness to shine from him.

At first he brought the little he had—pieces of candy, an orange, some writing paper.

Then—from as far away as Brooklyn and Boston—people heard what he was doing and sent him money.

Friends in town also made puddings, soups, and cakes for him to give those who could eat.

Often, it was Walt himself who fed the soldiers.

A few spoonfuls and a kind word could keep a man alive.

When I give I give myself.
—Walt Whitman, *Leaves of Grass*

There was so much Walt couldn't say in letters to his mother. The truth of war was not flags flying, but young men dying. So Walt looked beyond the wounds and sickness to the person *inside* the body.

He met their eyes with his, touched or held their hands, and read to them even if they seemed not to hear. Some hugged him about the neck, and Walt hugged them back.

In his mind, they were still strong and healthy, and could have been the sons he'd never had.

I am the poet of the Body and I am the poet of the Soul
—Walt Whitman, *Leaves of Grass*

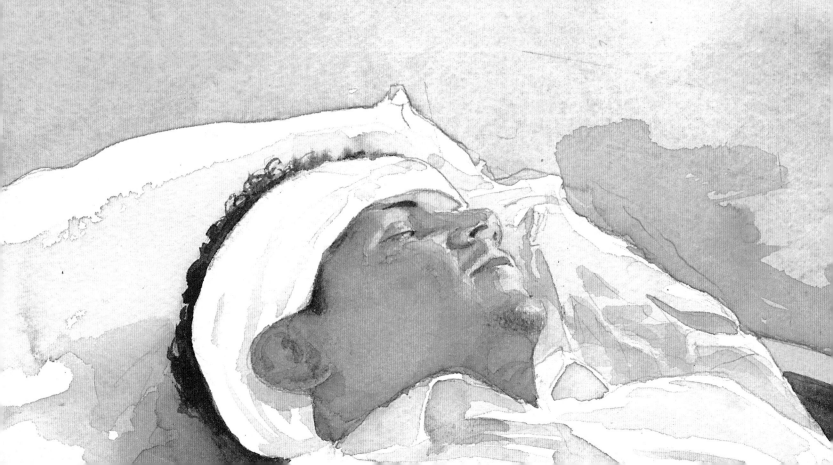

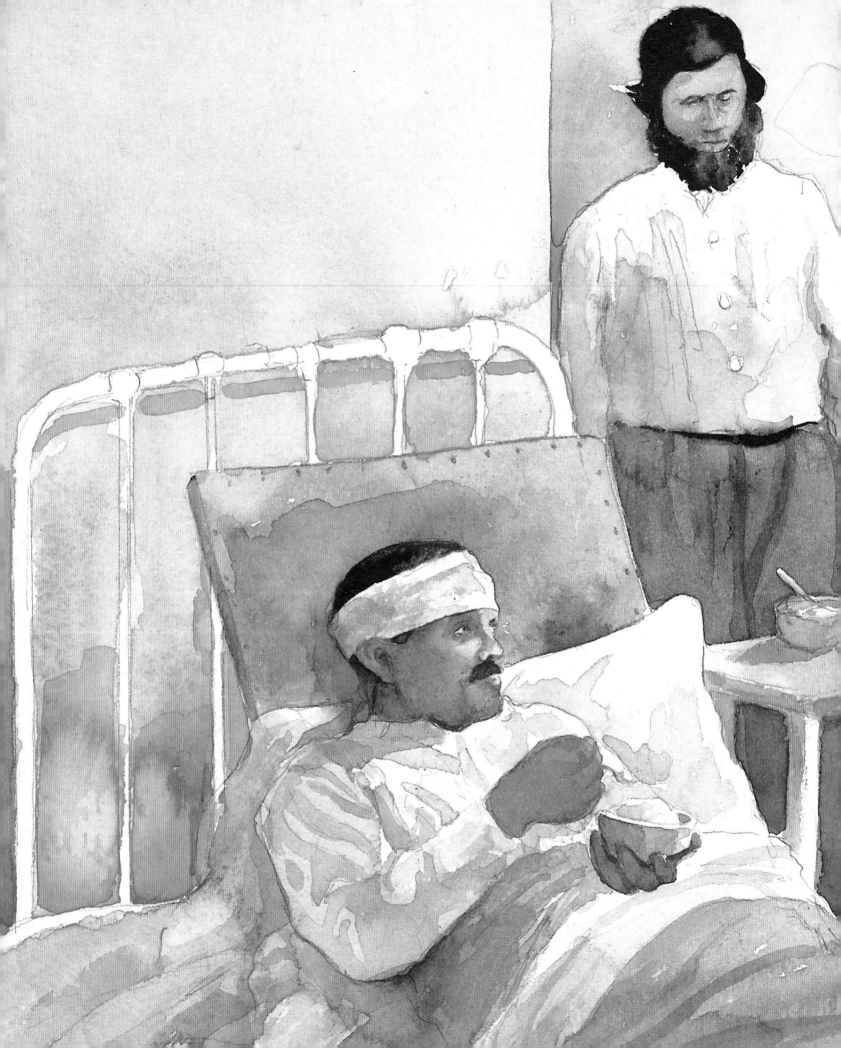

But there were also happy times, when Walt gathered the men to talk, read, or play guessing games.

When he'd dish out a few gallons of ice cream on hot summer days—to some who'd *never had a taste before!*

Laughter and ice cream were good medicine, too.

For Walt, walking through the wards was like walking through America, with soldiers from every state.

Some—with fever, frightened, far from home—relied on Walt's daily visits. He was the only friend they had in this strange place.

Once, a young man was afraid that Walt would leave his side *if the truth came out.*

When Walt asked what he meant, the man said he was a rebel soldier, on the *Southern* side.

Walt took his hand. *He already knew.*

There were no sides here.

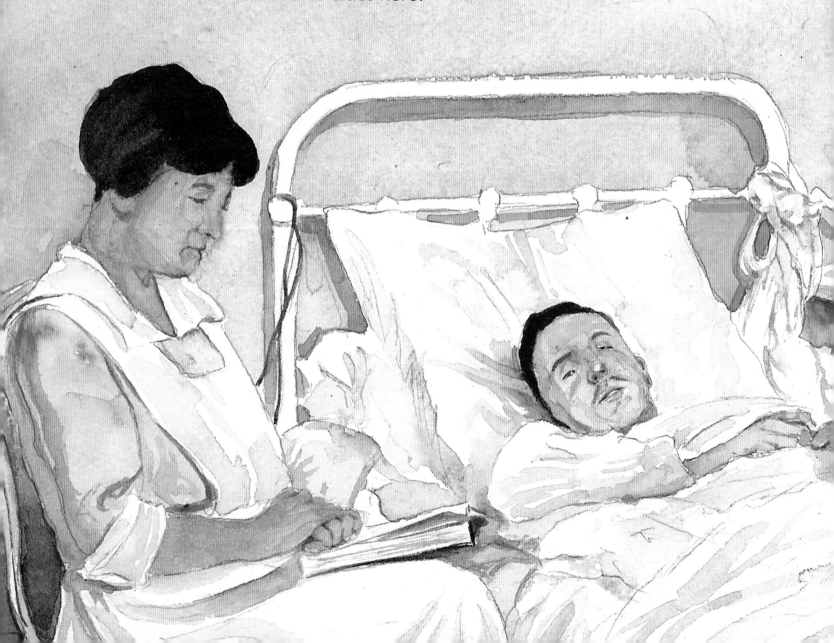

I am more than nurse,
more than parent or neighbor.
—Walt Whitman, *Leaves of Grass*

On nights like those, Walt walked slowly home.
The moon above—a beacon of golden light—shone bright
on both the North and South.
On all soldiers, all people.
And on the America that Walt would believe in for the rest of his life.

The moon gives you light,
And the bugles and the drums give you music.
And my heart, O my soldiers, my veterans,
My heart gives you love.

—Walt Whitman, Leaves of Grass

The Best of Friends

I hear America singing . . .
—Walt Whitman, *Leaves of Grass*

Walt Whitman was a man of great feeling. Close to his mother, sister, and brothers, he had many devoted friends and—in his later years—a national audience of readers who cherished the man and his work. Called the "Good Gray Poet" after the Civil War ended, Walt stood six feet tall, and was a striking presence with his long flowing hair and beard. As he moved throughout the wards of military hospitals from 1863 to 1865, the soldiers he visited thought of him as "Dear Brother," "Father," "the Old Man," and a "Santa Claus" of sorts, handing out small but much-appreciated gifts from his worn shoulder-pack. For years afterward, those who survived wrote grateful letters to the man who sat for hours beside their sickbeds, often naming their sons after him. They credited Walt with giving them hope during the dark hours when they lingered between life and death, unsure which way to go. And while it is believed that Walt may have visited nearly twenty-five thousand soldiers during his time in Washington, that number is less important than the size of Walt's heart.

The great beauty of Walt's life and work is that one mirrored the other. The deep love of nature, people, and the human body that fills his poems is the same love that brought him to the bedsides of the wounded day after day. Walt looked beyond the wounds or the color of a uniform to see himself in each soldier's face. He felt that fighting or killing anyone was fighting or killing yourself, since we are all basically the same, with mothers and fathers, children, sisters and brothers, homes we love, and Beauty all around us.

Walt's example of service during the Civil War is a story of *what one person can do*. He believed completely in the ideals that America stood for—friendship, equality, freedom, unity—and felt torn apart as his country was overcome by hatred and fear. What Walt did when he found his brother George (soon after the Battle of Fredericksburg) made it clear that he had the personal gifts—patience, compassion, an easygoing way with people—that would prove useful in helping the wounded. He wrote articles about the men and their struggles, but knew that he himself could do nothing to stop the war or the bloodshed. What he *could* do was act on a very simple, very human level, to comfort the sick, sit beside them as they left this world, send letters or messages to their families, and encourage them to keep living. In this work, Walt felt that he received much more than he ever gave, and called his service "the greatest privilege and satisfaction . . . and, of course, the most profound lesson of my life."

He was "only a friend" after all, in the very best of ways.

The United States themselves are essentially the greatest poem.
—Walt Whitman, in the 1855 preface to *Leaves of Grass*

Portrait of Walt Whitman by Civil War photographer
Mathew Brady, mid-1860s

"[N]o one person who assisted in the hospitals during the war accomplished so much good to the soldiers and for the Government as Mr. Whitman."
—Dr. Willard Bliss, chief surgeon at Armory Square Hospital, Washington, DC, during the Civil War

Armory Square Hospital, Ward K, Washington DC, 1862–65

Walt Whitman as Santa Claus

When Walt began his work in the hospitals, he soon fit the popular image of Saint Nick or Santa Claus with his long white hair and beard. Walt did his best to be "jolly" in his visits, handing out all sorts of gifts and treats from his shoulder pack. In it, he carried candy, biscuits, sugar, cans of condensed milk, jellies and preserves, tea, tobacco, pickles, stamps, envelopes, writing paper, socks, underwear, newspapers and books (though not all at the same time!). His pack—known as a *haversack* and often carried by soldiers themselves—was not very big, but limited only by the size of Walt's imagination. The original still exists in the collection of the Library of Congress.

Construction of the US Capitol Dome, early 1860s

Sources and Resources

All quotations used in the book can be found in the following sources.

Cohen, Matt, Ed Folsom, and Kenneth M. Price, eds. Walt Whitman Archive. whitmanarchive. org.

Morris, Roy. *The Better Angel: Walt Whitman in the Civil War.* New York: Oxford University Press, 2000.

Peck, Garrett. *Walt Whitman in Washington, D.C.: The Civil War and America's Great Poet.* Mount Pleasant, SC: Arcadia Publishing, 2015.

Traubel, Horace. *With Walt Whitman in Camden.* Boston: Small, Maynard & Company, 1906.

Whitman, Walt. *Leaves of Grass.* New York: HarperCollins, 2000.

———. *Song of Myself.* Nashville, TN: American Renaissance, 2010.

———. *Specimen Days in America.* London: Folio Society, 1979.

Acknowledgment

Much praise to the Walt Whitman Archive for the many labors of love that make it an invaluable resource and a lasting tribute.

Picture Credits

To the people of Ukraine, to whom we are all indebted —*GG*

Dedicated to those men and women who give the ultimate sacrifice for freedom —*EBL*

For information about permissions to reproduce selections from this book, please contact permissions@astrapublishinghouse.com.

Calkins Creek
An imprint of Astra Books for Young Readers,
a division of Astra Publishing House
astrapublishinghouse.com
Printed in China

ISBN: 978-1-63592-587-6 (hc)
ISBN: 978-1-63592-588-3 (eBook)
Library of Congress Control Number: 2023918686

First edition
10 9 8 7 6 5 4 3 2 1

Design by Barbara Grzeslo
The text is set in Futura Std medium.
The illustrations are done in watercolor on paper.